MW01379930

SilverTip

# The Rise and Fall of
# Mesopotamia

by D. R. Faust

Consultant: Caitlin Krieck, Social Studies Teacher and
Instructional Coach, The Lab School of Washington

BEARPORT
PUBLISHING

Minneapolis, Minnesota

## Bearport Publishing Company Product Development Team

President: Jen Jenson; Director of Product Development: Spencer Brinker; Managing Editor: Allison Juda; Associate Editor: Naomi Reich; Associate Editor: Tiana Tran; Art Director: Colin O'Dea; Designer: Kim Jones; Designer: Kayla Eggert; Product Development Assistant: Owen Hamlin

## Statement on Usage of Generative Artificial Intelligence

Bearport Publishing remains committed to publishing high-quality nonfiction books. Therefore, we restrict the use of generative AI to ensure accuracy of all text and visual components pertaining to a book's subject. See BearportPublishing.com for details.

*Library of Congress Cataloging-in-Publication Data*

Names: Faust, Daniel R., author.
Title: The rise and fall of Mesopotamia / by D.R. Faust.
Description: Minneapolis, Minnesota : Bearport Publishing Company, [2025] | Series: Ancient civilizations: need to know | Includes bibliographical references and index.
Identifiers: LCCN 2024005638 (print) | LCCN 2024005639 (ebook) | ISBN 9798892320474 (library binding) | ISBN 9798892325219 (paperback) | ISBN 9798892321808 (ebook)
Subjects: LCSH: Iraq–Civilization–To 634–Juvenile literature.
Classification: LCC DS70.62 .F38 2025 (print) | LCC DS70.62 (ebook) | DDC 935–dc23/eng/20240206
LC record available at https://lccn.loc.gov/2024005638
LC ebook record available at https://lccn.loc.gov/2024005639

For more information, write to Bearport Publishing, 5357 Penn Avenue South, Minneapolis, MN 55419.

# Contents

# A Different World

More than half of all people on Earth live in cities. **Urban** areas are often places where great growth and change happens. But there haven't always been cities. The first ones started thousands of years ago. They formed in an ancient place called Mesopotamia (*me-suh-puh-TAY-mee-uh*).

Mesopotamia was a region in southwest Asia. This area is now called the Middle East. Most of the land once known as Mesopotamia is part of modern Iraq.

# Between Two Rivers

The name *Mesopotamia* means land between two rivers. These two rivers are the Tigris and Euphrates. People first settled this region in about 10,000 BCE. They gathered along the banks of the rivers. These waterways made the land very **fertile**.

Mesopotamia is sometimes called the Cradle of **Civilization**. It was the first place humans settled for a long period. Being together let people create a shared **culture**. They formed the first civilizations.

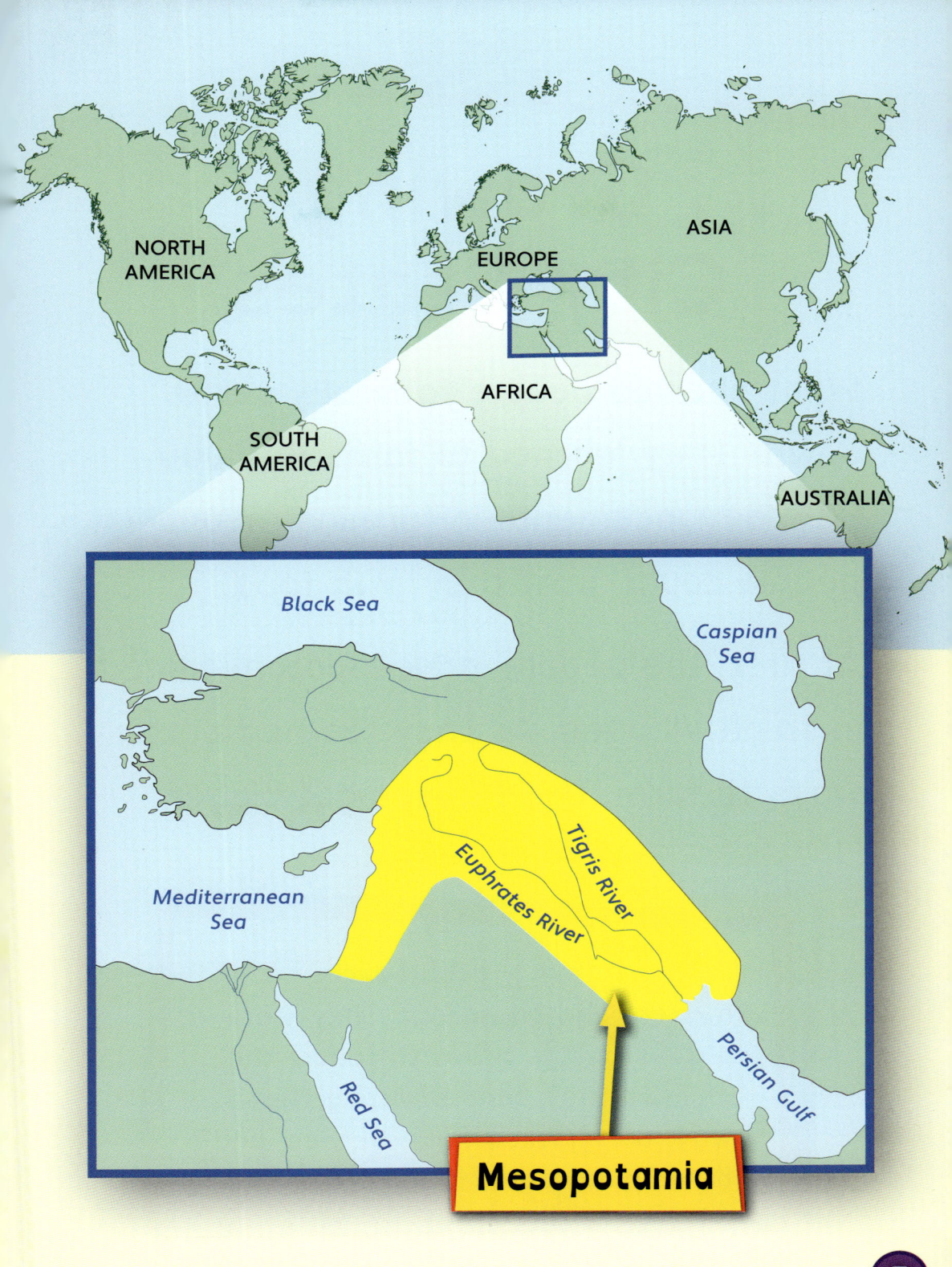

NORTH
AMERICA

EUROPE

ASIA

AFRICA

SOUTH
AMERICA

AUSTRALIA

Black Sea

Caspian
Sea

Mediterranean
Sea

Euphrates River

Tigris River

Red Sea

Persian Gulf

**Mesopotamia**

# Growing City-States

What allowed people to finally settle down? They learned to farm. By 5000 BCE, advancements in farming meant people could grow their own food.

At first, the people in Mesopotamia lived in small villages. As they learned better ways to farm, the villages got bigger.

Before farming, people were hunters and gatherers. They were always on the move to follow the animals they hunted. Along the way, they picked nuts, berries, and other plants that grew in the wild.

Over time, these villages continued to expand. Some became large, powerful city-states. The first of these city-states were formed by the Sumerian people in about 4000 BCE.

The Sumerians created governments to run their communities. Each city-state had its own king and ruled itself.

Sumerian city-states controlled the southern part of Mesopotamia. This area was known as Sumer. Sumer's important city-states included Eridu (ER-i-doo), Uruk (OO-rook), and Ur (OOR).

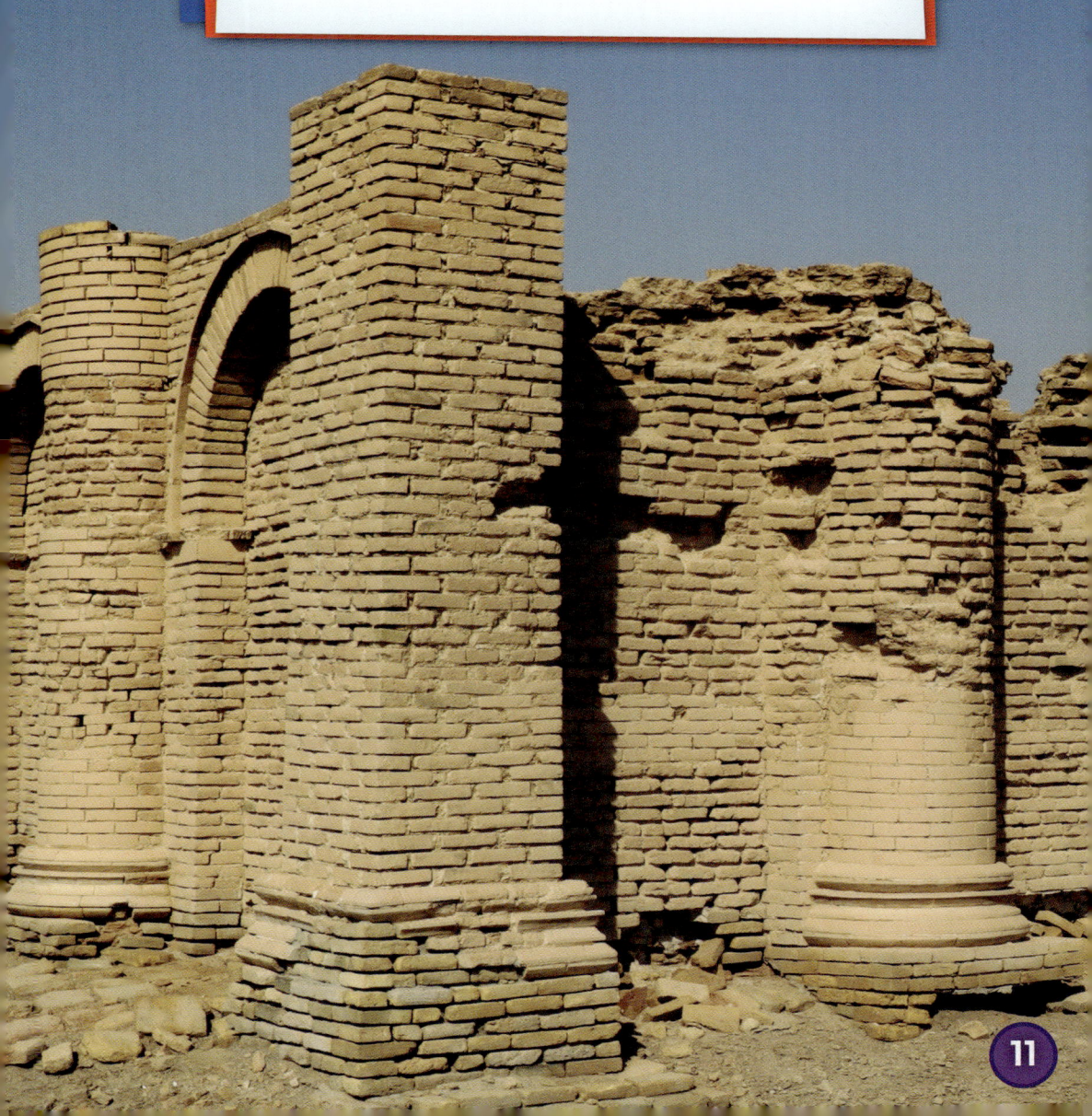

# Wheels and Writing

The Sumerians also made many early tools. They invented the wheel in 3500 BCE. At first, wheels were used to make pottery.

The Sumerians created a system of writing around 3300 BCE. They drew symbols on clay tablets. Ancient records show writing about laws and business deals.

The people of Mesopotamia also wrote stories. They told tales about gods and heroes. *The Epic of Gilgamesh* was written around 2000 BCE. This long, storytelling poem is about the adventures of a king.

This writing system was known as cuneiform (kyoo-NAY-ih-*form*).

# Warring City-States

Civilization continued to advance. But there was no single ruling power in Mesopotamia. This led to conflict. Sometimes, city-states would fight. Each wanted control of land. They would also fight over **trade routes**. The first recorded war happened in 2700 BCE.

City-states were not always fighting. Sometimes, two or more worked together and shared power. This led to some city-states forming **regional** states.

# Rise and Fall

The Sumerian city-states were powerful, but they faced challengers over the years. Northern Mesopotamia was ruled by the Akkadian people. In 2300 BCE, Akkadian king Sargon the Great wanted more land. He took over Sumer. This was the start of the Akkadian **Empire**.

The Akkadians and Sumerians were a lot alike. One major difference was their language. After the Akkadians took over, the Sumerian language disappeared.

Sargon the Great

For more than 200 years, the Akkadians held control. They grew their empire to the east, west, and south. Then in 2100 BCE, the Sumerians returned to power. After 200 more years, the Assyrians replaced the Sumerians. The Assyrians controlled Mesopotamia from 1900 until 1792 BCE.

The Assyrian army was very powerful. It was the first to use iron weapons. Assyrian soldiers were also some of the first to use horses in battle.

# A King's Code

In 1792 BCE, a man named Hammurabi (ha-muh-RAH-bee) came to power. He controlled Babylon, a city-state in the south. Soon, Babylon took over Mesopotamia.

Hammurabi created 282 laws for the empire. Today, these laws are called the Code of Hammurabi. This is one of the oldest recorded sets of laws.

Babylon was once the most powerful city in the world. It was also the largest. More than 100,000 people lived there at its peak.

Hammurabi's laws
were displayed
in public for
everyone to see.

# A Great Empire

For hundreds of years, the Babylonians and the Assyrians fought for control of Mesopotamia. At the same time, the Persian Empire was growing. This civilization was started around 550 BCE by Cyrus the Great. Cyrus soon spread his empire into Mesopotamia. This made the Persian Empire the largest on Earth.

The Persian Empire was more than 3,000 miles (4,800 km) across. It controlled all of Mesopotamia. It also had power over the land that is modern Egypt, Turkey, and Israel.

Cyrus the Great

23

The Persian Empire was too large for a single king to rule. It was divided into dozens of smaller regions. Each was ruled by a governor who answered to the king. These governors **enforced** the king's laws. They collected taxes from the people.

The Persians built many roads to connect their empire. They used the roads to deliver messages. This was an early version of a mail service.

Persepolis was once the capital of the Persian Empire.

# All Greek to Me

In 490 BCE, the Persian Empire attacked Greece. The Persians wanted control over those powerful city-states. They had some early success. But in 334 BCE, Alexander the Great helped Greece take over the Persian Empire. This marked the end of the last great ancient Mesopotamian civilization.

Before they fell, the Persians had a massive empire. They were the first to spread across three continents. Their empire included land in Africa, Asia, and Europe.

# Mesopotamia Timeline

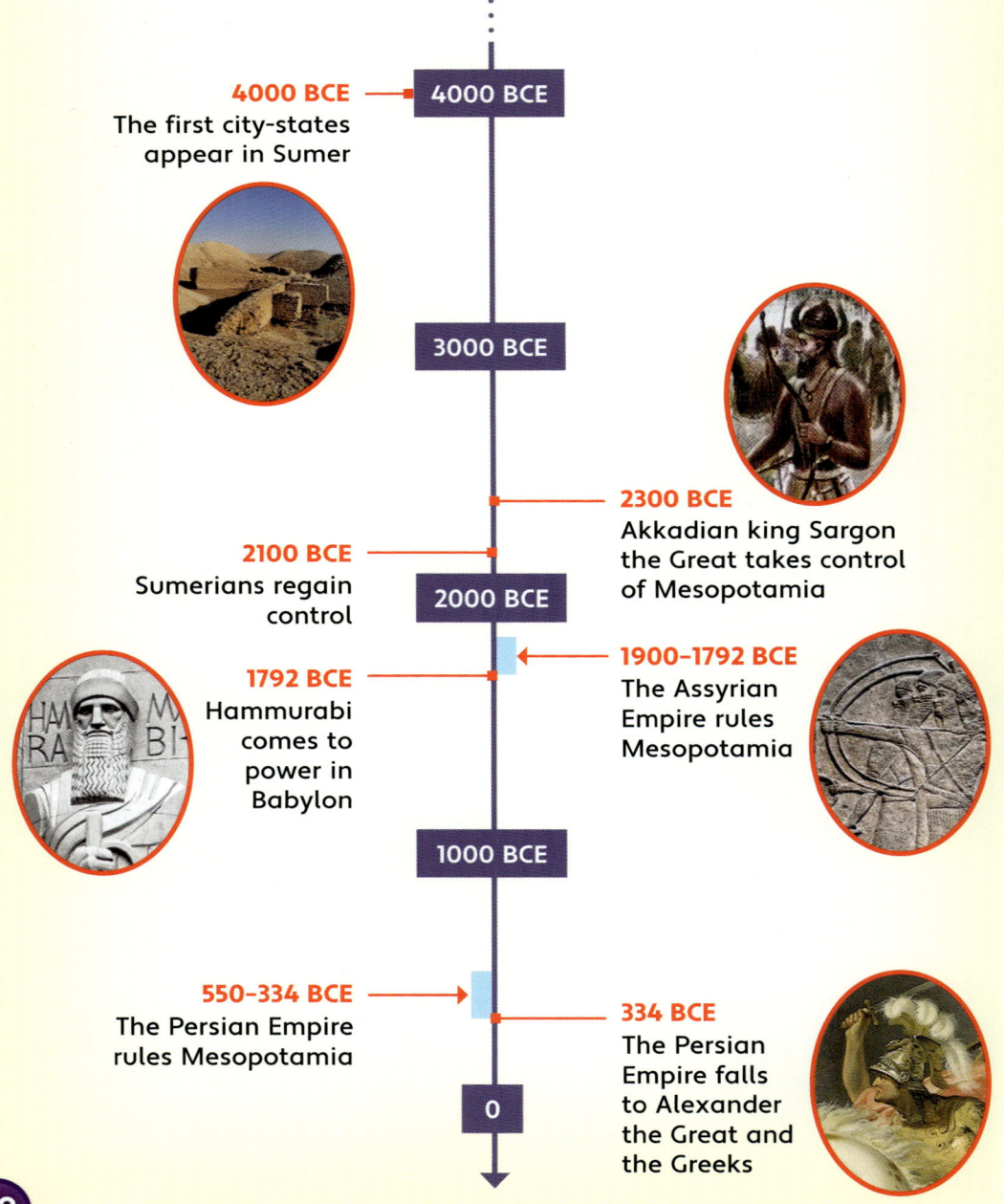

**4000 BCE** — 4000 BCE
The first city-states appear in Sumer

3000 BCE

**2300 BCE**
Akkadian king Sargon the Great takes control of Mesopotamia

**2100 BCE**
Sumerians regain control

2000 BCE

**1900–1792 BCE**
The Assyrian Empire rules Mesopotamia

**1792 BCE**
Hammurabi comes to power in Babylon

1000 BCE

**550–334 BCE**
The Persian Empire rules Mesopotamia

**334 BCE**
The Persian Empire falls to Alexander the Great and the Greeks

0

## ★ SilverTips for REVIEW

Review what you've learned. Use the text to help you.

### Define key terms

Akkadians                    Persian Empire

Assyrians                    Sumerians

Babylon

### Check for understanding

What allowed people to start settling in Mesopotamia?

Which region did the first city-states appear in? What was one of their key accomplishments?

Explain how the Cradle of Civilization eventually lost power.

### Think deeper

How would your life be different without the influence of ancient civilizations from Mesopotamia?

---

## ★ SilverTips on TEST-TAKING

- **Make a study plan.** Ask your teacher what the test is going to cover. Then, set aside time to study a little bit every day.

- **Read all the questions carefully.** Be sure you know what is being asked.

- **Skip any questions** you don't know how to answer right away. Mark them and come back later if you have time.

# Glossary

**civilization** a large group of people who share the same history and way of life

**culture** the ideas, customs, and way of life for a group of people

**empire** a large region ruled by a single person or government

**enforced** made sure laws or rules were followed

**fertile** able to help plants grow

**regional** relating to a particular area

**trade routes** roads, paths, or waterways traveled by people bringing goods from one place to another

**urban** having to do with a city

# Read More

**Finan, Catherine C.** *Mesopotamia (X-treme Facts: Ancient History).* Minneapolis: Bearport Publishing Company, 2022.

**Levy, Janey.** *The Advances of Ancient Mesopotamia (That's Ancient!).* New York: Gareth Stevens Publishing, 2022.

**Reynolds, Donna.** *Ancient Mesopotamia Revealed (Unearthing Ancient Civilizations).* New York: Cavendish Square Publishing, 2023.

# Learn More Online

1. Go to **www.factsurfer.com** or scan the QR code below.

2. Enter "**Civilizations Mesopotamia**" into the search box.

3. Click on the cover of this book to see a list of websites.

# Index

# About the Author

D. R. Faust is a freelance writer of fiction and nonfiction. They live in Queens, NY.